What's Different About You?

Medical Conditions and Disabilities Explained for Caring Kids

Copyright © 2014 by Heather Steiger

ISBN-13: 978-1500701468

ISBN-10: 1500701467

Editor: Cherie Frankenberg

Author's Note: This is a work of nonfiction. The author has received consent for use of names and/or pictures.

Fonts copyright of DJ Inkers, Diane J.Hook License #0614200371

Graphics license purchased 2014

A note to the parent or teacher....

As a teacher and a mom of a child with special needs, I believe there is a lack of literature to educate young and impressionable minds about mild and severe disabilities as well as a variety of medical conditions that some of our youngest children face. Most books that address differences avoid topics that many kids question and need answers about. Until we begin conversing and directly teaching about these topics, children will continue to be uneducated, form incorrect opinions and lack understanding. Everyone is less intimidated by others who are different if they have more exposure and an understanding of those differences.

Whether you are reading this book to a child because there is a person in their life this book relates to, or you're just reading it to widen the range of understanding and compassion your audience member has, the purpose of this book is to begin a dialogue. Use the pictures and vocabulary words as a springboard for conversation. It's never too early to begin talking and answering questions about these subjects. Doing so creates a world filled with more care, concern and consideration of others.

Sincerely,
Heather Steiger

What's Different About You?

Medical Conditions and Disabilities Explained for Caring Kids

"Not everything that is faced can be changed, but nothing can be changed until it is faced."

-James Baldwin

Some children are boys and some are girls.

When those children grow older, they become men and women.

Some kids have golden tan skin and others have black skin. Some have white skin and others have brown. The reason you have skin is so that your bones and insides are covered and protected. Skin colors are different so that we can each be more unique and show our ancestry.

Some people have short hair, some have long hair and some people are bald. Some people have light hair, some people have dark hair. Hair can be curly, straight or frizzy.

What kind of hair do you have?

Some faces are soft to the touch while others are rough. Some faces have freckles or dots. Other people have wrinkles on their faces because they are older.

What does your face look like?

Some people have smaller bodies while others are larger.

This is
what a big foot
looks like next to
a little foot.

Some people can walk and run using their legs, while others get around in a wheelchair or use a walker to help them. There are many different reasons that a child or adult might not be able to use their legs to walk. If a person uses a wheelchair or walker, they can ride or walk up a ramp.

Wheelchairs can be motorized or manual. If the wheelchair is motorized, a battery in the wheelchair makes it move. If the wheelchair is manual, a person uses their hands and arms to push the wheels so that the chair can move in all directions.

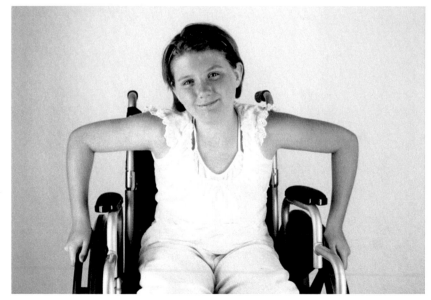

Most people have four limbs. The word "limb" is a fancy word for an arm or leg. While most people have two arms and two legs, others might be missing one or more. The person could have been born without a limb or have been in an accident. You would be amazed at what people can do even when they are missing one or more of their limbs!

What things do you do with your arms and legs?

This is Doug and his hand. He had an accident and lost the tip of his finger. He still uses his hand like he always did before the accident. He drives a bus for school children. Even though Doug's hand was normal for most of his life, he learned how to adapt with his new hand very quickly.

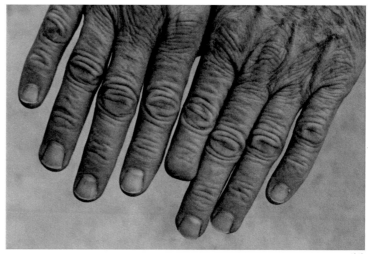

While some people can see with their eyes, others can't. People who can't see with their eyes use their ears, nose and touch to see their way around. They might use a cane to help navigate the way. If a person can't see at all, he or she is known as being blind. If a person can't see very well, they could be visually impaired. Millions of people in the world have visual impairments that are easily corrected...with glasses.

Some people use ears to hear someone talk or to hear what is going on around them. Other people can't hear well or can't hear at all. Hearing aids help people who need to make the sounds around them louder. If a person can't hear at all and is completely deaf, they might read lips and use sign language to communicate.

A cochlear implant allows some adults and children, like Meredith, to hear.

Austin uses a hearing aid to make sounds louder.

What tools and body parts do you use to communicate?

Some people eat with their mouths while other people can't. If you can't eat with your mouth, your body still needs fuel. Fortunately, there is a tube that can deliver food right into a person's stomach! The food is liquid and helps the person grow and have energy just like the kind of food that is eaten off a plate.

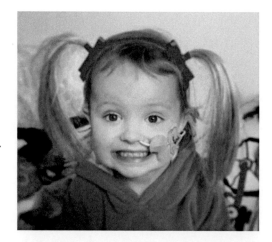

Sometimes this tube goes in through a person's nose. The tube is held on by a piece of tape and is called an NG tube. If the person will need to be fed through a tube for a long time or forever, the doctor can place a tube into the person's stomach. This is called a G tube. The food can be pushed into the stomach by a pump or it can flow in by gravity. No matter how people eat, they always feel full when they are finished!

How and what do you like to eat?

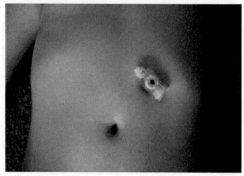

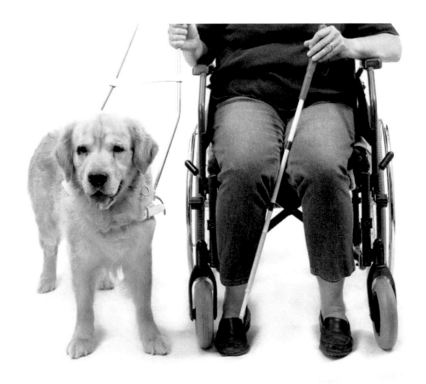

Some people walk alone, with a friend or with someone in their family. Other people walk with a dog that is trained to be their special helper. These dogs are called service dogs. They help a person safely cross the street, open doors and retrieve items when told. Many types of animals can be used for service including horses and monkeys, but dogs are used most often.

Should you pet a service animal when it is working?

No, you can look and smile, but let the animal do its job.

Reading, writing or math can be hard for some people to learn and easy for others. That is because everyone has a different brain and we all learn things at different speeds.

What things are easy for you to do or learn?
What things are hard?

Some people like to talk to other people and can make friends easily. Other people have a hard time knowing what to say at the right time or how to talk to others. One condition that makes communicating difficult is called autism. Many children and adults have autism. Just because people have difficulty communicating doesn't mean they aren't friendly. It just means that they make friendships in a different way and they might be more comfortable doing some things by themselves.

What kinds of things do you like to do alone?

What do you like to do with a friend?

Sometimes people can be born with a medical condition or develop it later. When a person has a medical condition, they have to visit the doctor or hospital more often. They may even have to do things at home that normally would only be done in an office. For example, people with diabetes have to check their blood to make sure it has the right amount of sugar. They might have to give themselves a shot or check their blood by pricking their finger and putting the blood into a small hand-held computer.

Alexis is a third grader who has diabetes. She has to test her blood sugar around 10 times a day. She does this by pricking her finger. If her blood sugar is low, she needs to eat food; but if her blood sugar is high, she needs something called insulin. Alexis has an insulin pump that delivers the medicine directly into her body. If Alexis didn't have her pump, she would have to get a shot of insulin many times each day.

Managing diabetes is a constant juggling act for Alexis and her parents but it doesn't stop her from doing the same things as other children her age. She rides horses, dances, swims and plays with her siblings and friends.

Alexis has a team of 70 people who walk with her in the "JDRF Walk to Cure Diabetes" each year. Since she has been diagnosed, she has raised more than $20,000 to help find a cure. One day Alexis hopes she can say, "I *used to* have diabetes."

Alexis' Insulin Pump

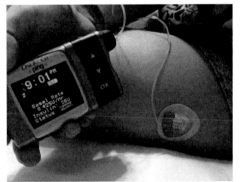

Another medical condition is called Cystic Fibrosis. This condition affects a person's lungs and can make it hard to breathe. It is very important that the classroom and environment of a child with cystic fibrosis are clean so germs that cause sickness are not spread. Sometimes children with cystic fibrosis wear a vest that vibrates to help clear the mucus in their lungs. They might even have to get medicine at home or in school through an IV. If this happens, they will have a bag of medicine that hangs on a pole. There is a line that the medicine flows through. This is usually an antibiotic used to clear up infection.

What do you do to keep your body in good health?

Brianna takes a pulmonary function test to measure the amount of air that goes in and out of her lungs. Since the cystic fibrosis makes Brianna have frequent infections in her lungs, she has had to take a lot of antibiotics. This has caused her to lose her hearing. She used hearing aids for a very long time but now wears a cochlear implant.

Meet Jack. Jack's brain didn't form properly so when he was born he had many seizures. A seizure is when the brain sends the wrong message and makes the body move in ways it can't control. If a person has seizures more than just a few times, they are often diagnosed as having epilepsy, just like Jack. Doctors use brain surgery and medications to reduce or stop seizures. Both of these methods have helped Jack.

Jack has also had a stroke. A stroke is a brain injury that makes a part of the brain stop working. Jack cannot talk and he uses a wheelchair to get around. He eats food but if he doesn't eat enough, his mom and dad can feed him through his G tube. He smiles all the time and loves to hug and snuggle.

Some children are born with a syndrome. This means they might look, learn or act different. There are many different types of syndromes and each syndrome has its own characteristics.

Meet Joe. Joe has Down syndrome. He was born with this condition. Joe likes to play sports and hang out with his friends. Every year, hundreds of people gather at Coney Island in Cincinnati, Ohio to walk, run and swim at the "Tri for Joe" to support all people with Down syndrome. The race was named after this famous boy!

Maxime is a strong young man who has CHARGE syndrome. Children with this syndrome can have life-threatening conditions, but with advances in medical care, many children with CHARGE survive and become healthier. Some of Maxime's differences can be seen, like the hearing aids he wears. Other differences can't be seen because they are under his skin. In Maxime's case, he was born with a special heart that did not work properly. He had surgery on his heart when he was seven. Now he can run, jump and dance like everyone else! He loves horses and knows quite a few different languages.

Lianna has a condition called cerebral palsy, or CP. Over 500,000 people in the world have CP. Did you know that different parts of our brain control different things? We have a speech center which is the place that creates the words we think and say. We also have a motor center. This is the part of the brain that controls our movements, including making our arms and legs move properly.

When someone has cerebral palsy, their motor center, the place in the brain that controls movements, is damaged. If a large part of the motor center is damaged, it might mean the person cannot walk or talk. If only a small part is damaged, only a bit of their body might be affected.

Sometimes we can look at someone and tell that they are different. Other times we can't. But whether you can see it or not, EVERYONE is different. The one common bond we all share is that we all want to be cared about, loved and appreciated for what we can do!

What can you do to make others feel loved, cared for and appreciated?

Index

This book is dedicated to all

children with special needs or medical needs,

including my own son, Jack, who is pictured in this book.

It is also dedicated to all these children's caretakers, including

parents, grandparents, therapists/teachers, nurses and doctors.

47994560R00018